MW01131520

THE WIDE OPEN GRASSLANDS

A Web of Life

Philip Johansson

 Enslow Publishers, Inc.

40 Industrial Road	PO Box 38
Box 398	Aldershot
Berkeley Heights, NJ 07922	Hants GU12 6BP
USA	UK

http://www.enslow.com

Library of Congress Cataloging-in-Publication Data

Johansson, Philip.
    The wide open grasslands : a web of life / Philip Johansson.
        p. cm. — (A world of biomes)
    Includes index.
    ISBN 0-7660-2201-3 (hardcover)
    1. Grassland ecology—Juvenile literature. [1. Grasslands. 2. Grassland ecology. 3. Ecology.] I. Title.
    QH541.5.P7J63 2004
    577.4—dc22

                                                                    2003025433

Printed in the United States of America

10 9 8 7 6 5 4 3 2 1

To Our Readers: We have done our best to make sure all Internet Addresses in this book were active and appropriate when we went to press. However, the author and the publisher have no control over and assume no liability for the material available on those Internet sites or on other Web sites they may link to. Any comments or suggestions can be sent by e-mail to comments@enslow.com or to the address on the back cover.

Photo Credits: © Adam Jones/Visuals Unlimited, Inc., pp. 30, 32; © 2002–2004 Art Today, Inc., pp. 9, 16, 26; © 1999 Artville, LLC, pp. 10–11; © Corel Corporation, p. 4; © Fritz Polking/Visuals Unlimited, Inc., p. 43; © Gerald and Buff Corsi/Visuals Unlimited, Inc., pp. 15, 22, 37; © Gill Lopez-Espina/Visuals Unlimited, Inc., p. 34; © Inga Spence/Visuals Unlimited, Inc., pp. 13, 20, 31 (top); © Jack Ballard/Visuals Unlimited, Inc., p. 38; © Joe McDonald/Visuals Unlimited, Inc., pp. 7, 28, 31 (bottom), 39, 41, 44; Rob Bowen: Lady Bird Johnson Wildflower Center, pp. 5, 27; © Leroy Simon/Visuals Unlimited, Inc., p. 35; © Richard Thom/Visuals Unlimited, Inc., pp. 2–3 (background), 29; © Theo Allofs/Visuals Unlimited, Inc., p. 18; © Tom Brakefield/CORBIS, pp. 2, 40.

Illustration Credits: *Heck's Pictorial Archive of Art and Architecture*, except for Dover Publications, Inc., pp. 12, 21, 33.

Cover Photos: © Gerald and Buff Corsi/Visuals Unlimited (top left); © 2002–2004 Art Today, Inc. (top right); © Beth Davidson/Visuals Unlimited (bottom left); © Adam Jones/Visuals Unlimited (bottom right).

Dave Balfour is a conservation biologist with KwaZulu-Natal Nature Conservation Service, studying the impact of large herbivores on the vegetation of Hluhluwe-iMfolozi Park, South Africa. The volunteers depicted in Chapter 1 are from Earthwatch Institute, a nonprofit organization. Earthwatch supports field science and conservation through the participation of the public. See *www.earthwatch.org* for more information.

Table of *Table of* CONTENTS

Zebras live in the grasslands of Africa.

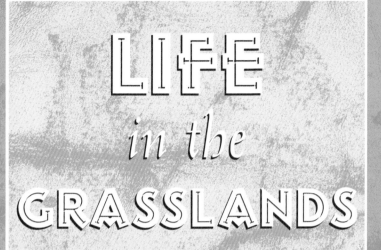

LIFE in the GRASSLANDS

Scientist Dave Balfour and two volunteer field assistants have been out since the first light of dawn. They are walking a straight line across a rolling grassland in South Africa. Spreading acacia trees dot the land, which is covered with a blanket of grass. The grass is green, yellow, and tan as far as they can see.

◇ 5 ◇

The dry air is just warming up and smells faintly of animal dung. Insects are buzzing all around in the bright sunlight. Finally, they find what they are looking for: a herd of zebras.

"I count twelve of them, eating among the brush there," whispers Balfour. "How many do you get?" He and the two assistants quietly watch the group of zebras from the top of a hill. They are especially interested in what the zebras eat.

Zebras have a big appetite for grass. Like other grass eaters, they are called grazers. Zebras eat many tough grasses that other grazers avoid. The kinds of grasses they leave behind for other animals to eat have a big impact on the grassland biome. Dave Balfour is part of a team of scientists researching what zebras are eating, and how much, in Hluhluwe-iMfolozi Park, South Africa.

Counting Zebras

"There are two more, hidden to the right," says one of the field assistants, peering through binoculars.

They all agree on a total of fourteen zebras.

They use an instrument called a range finder to figure out how far away the herd is. They find the direction of the group using a compass. These measurements will help them place the herd on a map later. Once they have made these notes, they observe what the zebras eat and where they are headed.

"They are eating the older grass, including long, tough stems and seed heads," says Balfour, watching the zebras through binoculars. "That will open up this land to pickier grazers, like wildebeests, which prefer to eat short grasses."

Dave Balfour and his assistants watched the zebras eat in the grasslands.

The team finishes their work, then packs up to continue walking. They will walk six miles (ten kilometers), before the heat of midday. They will see much more wildlife, including a few rhinos and a group of giraffes gathered around a clump of acacia trees. In just one morning, they will watch many animals most people see only in books.

Learning From Zebras

Balfour and his team have been studying zebras, elephants, rhinos, and other wildlife in the South African park for many years. They want to learn more about how the different kinds of large plant-eaters in this rich grassland live together. The research will help park managers figure out how many zebras or other types of wildlife can successfully live in one area. They can control their numbers to keep grazers and other plant eaters from damaging the grassland that all the wildlife depends on.

What Is a Biome?

Grasslands are one kind of biome. A biome is a large region of Earth where certain plants and animals live. They survive there because they are well suited to the soils, landscape, and climate found in that area. The climate is a result of the temperatures and amounts of rainfall that usually occur during a year.

As the team finished their day, they observed giraffes standing under an acacia tree.

Each biome has plants that may not be found in other biomes. Trees grow in forests, but not in deserts. Cacti grow in deserts, but not in the tundra. The animals that eat these plants help form the living

LEGEND

Tundra

Taiga

Temperate forest

Grassland

Desert

Rain forest

Chaparral

Mountain zone

Polar ice

Biomes

communities of a biome. Exploring biomes is a good way to begin to understand how these communities work. In this book you will learn about the grassland biome and the plants and animals that live there.

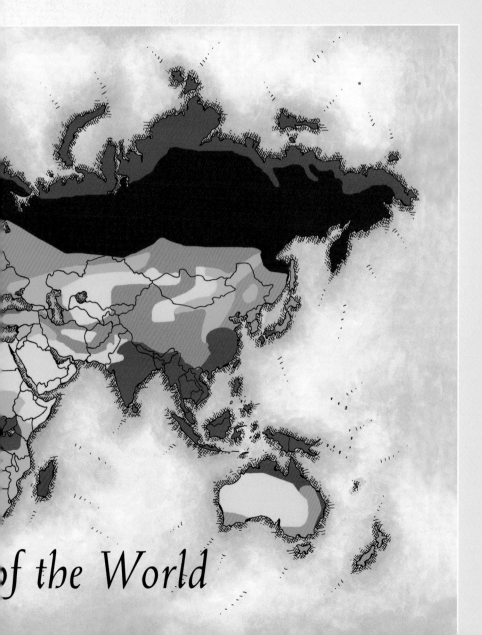

of the World

Chapter 2

The GRASSLAND BIOME

You can find grasslands—vast oceans of grass and other low-growing plants—on every continent except Antarctica. Grasslands cover one fifth of the world's land. They are important areas for many kinds of wildlife, and for humans as well.

Although grass is the first thing you will notice there, grasslands often include many other types of plants. Wildflowers mix in with the grasses, sprinkling the view with colors in the spring. Small bushes sometimes grow among the grasses, and trees stand tall along streams and rivers. Seed-eating birds cling to the waving stalks of grass. Grazing mammals and other plant eaters thrive on the carpet of plant food.

Grasslands in North America are called prairies. In Europe and Asia, they are called steppes. In South America, there are the pampas. These are all examples of temperate grasslands, which grow in cooler areas of the world.

Grasslands in Africa are called velds and savannas, which together cover about half of this large continent.

Prairie grass covers a grassland in Wyoming (top).

In the spring, wildflowers blanket a California grassland.

Savannas, such as where Dave Balfour studies zebras, are grasslands scattered with trees. Savannas and velds are examples of tropical or subtropical grasslands— they grow closer to the equator.

All of these grasslands have one thing in common: a large carpet of grasses blowing in the wind. The local weather patterns allow the grasses to grow well.

Grassland Weather

Grasslands usually grow in regions that are too dry for forests to grow, but not dry enough to be desert. It is not surprising, then, that grasslands are often found on the land between deserts and forests. In Africa, for example, grasslands can be found in the area between the Sahara Desert in the north and rain forests to the south.

Most grasslands get between 10 and 30 inches (25 and 76 centimeters) of rain each year. Temperate grasslands may get some of their precipitation in the form of snow. Most of the rain in tropical grasslands

comes during a wet season. This is followed by several
months with little or no rain. The season of harsh, dry
weather would wilt the seedlings of many forest plants
and make it hard for most trees to survive. But many
grasses are able to withstand these conditions.

Grasslands face different temperatures, depending
on where they are located. North American prairies
can reach extreme temperatures of −40 degrees
Fahrenheit (−40 degrees Celsius) in the winter and

*Rain clouds
gather over
this tropical
grassland
during the
wet season.*

THE WIDE OPEN GRASSLANDS

Grazers, such as this pronghorn antelope, eat grasses and keep the growth low.

100 degrees Fahrenheit (38 degrees Celsius) in the summer. African savanna grasslands experience milder temperatures, with a monthly average of 64 degrees Fahrenheit (18 degrees Celsius). The temperature is not as important in shaping grasslands as the cycle of wet and dry weather and other factors such as fire.

Grass Growth

In many grasslands, grazing animals help keep the grass growth low. Grazers, such as pronghorn antelope, eat certain taller grasses, which prevents tall grass from crowding out other grasses. Grazers allow the grassland to have a wide variety of grasses and other plants. This variety, in turn, can feed more kinds of animals.

◇ **16** ◇

Other animals, such as elephants and rhinos, eat shrubs and other woody plants. These animals are called browsers. They prevent many of these woody plants from growing larger and shading out the grasses.

Many grasslands rely on fire to keep them healthy. In tropical grasslands, fires usually occur in the dry season, when grasses are tall and parched. The fires eliminate young trees, shrubs, and other plants that might otherwise rise over the grassland. Grass stalks burn as well, but the grass shoots survive below the ground.

Fires also do one other thing that is especially important in the tropics: They help cycle nutrients by releasing them back into the soil. Nutrients are chemicals that plants need to live and grow. After a fire, the nutrients that were in the dry grass stalks return to the soil. They will be available for the roots of new grasses the next rainy season.

Fires are important to grasslands. They help release nutrients so that new grasses can grow.

The Fertile Ground

Grasslands in northern regions, such as the prairies of North America and the steppes of Europe and Asia, have deep, fertile soil. Years and years of fallen grasses and other plants have added nutrients to the soil. Each year, the plant material

breaks down, or decomposes. It becomes dark soil
that is rich in nutrients. There is not much rainfall to
wash all these nutrients out.

The rich soils of prairies and steppes make them
ideal for farmers to grow crops. Many grasslands
have been changed into farmland. In the United
States, there was once 1.5 million square miles of
prairie. Now, only a fraction of that is left.

Tropical grassland soils are not usually so
fertile. They tend to get more rain than temperate
grasslands. The rain washes away nutrients. The layer
of decomposed grasses is not very thick. Tropical
grasslands need regular fires to help release precious
nutrients back into the soil.

✓ **More than grass:** Grasslands also include many kinds of wildflowers. Some also have bushes and trees near rivers.

✓ **Many names:** Grasslands are also called prairies, steppes, savannas, velds, and pampas.

✓ **Varying temperatures:** Temperate grasslands can have a wide range of temperatures, from –40 degrees Fahrenheit (–40 Celsius) in the winter to 100 degrees Fahrenheit (38 degrees Celsius) in the summer. Tropical grasslands usually have a more constant, mild temperature.

GRASSLAND FACTS

✓ **Natural maintenance:** Grasslands rely on fires and browsing animals to eliminate bushes and small trees and to maintain the variety of plants.

✓ **Dry season:** Most grasslands get between 10 and 30 inches (25 and 76 centimeters) of rain. Tropical grasslands have long dry seasons with no rain at all.

✓ **Diverse soils:** Temperate grasslands have rich soils, but tropical grasslands usually have poor soils.

GRASSLAND COMMUNITIES

Grasslands

are made up of living
communities of plants and
animals. Communities are the
groups of living things found
together in a place. Each living thing
has a role in the community. Some
plants and animals depend on others.

Energy Flow in the Grassland

Grassland plants, such as prairie cordgrass and coneflower, trap the sun's energy for their food. They use the energy to make sugars from carbon dioxide (a gas in the air) and water from the soil. They store the sugars and use the energy later when they need it to build new leaves, stems, roots, and flowers. Some animals, such as bison, prairie dogs, and grasshoppers, eat these plants. Animals that eat

only plants are called herbivores. Herbivores get their energy from plants. Other animals, called carnivores, eat herbivores. Coyotes, gopher snakes, and golden eagles are carnivores. Carnivores get their energy from eating the meat of other animals. Some animals, such as red foxes, eat both plants and animals. They are called omnivores.

Soil animals and fungi get their energy from plants and animals after they die. They break down the dead plants and animals and release nutrients back into the soil. Earthworms, beetles, fungi, microbes, and other soil life do this job. They are called decomposers.

The Food Web

The flow of energy through the grassland from the sun to plants to herbivores to carnivores and decomposers follows a pattern called a food web. Like a spider's web, it is a complicated network of who eats whom. The web connects all the plants and

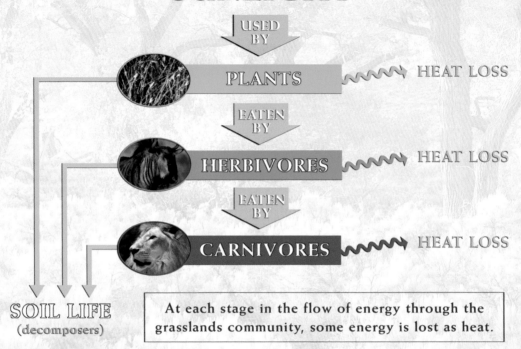

SUNLIGHT

USED BY

PLANTS ~~~~~ HEAT LOSS

EATEN BY

HERBIVORES ~~~~~ HEAT LOSS

EATEN BY

CARNIVORES ~~~~~ HEAT LOSS

SOIL LIFE
(decomposers)

At each stage in the flow of energy through the grasslands community, some energy is lost as heat.

animals of a particular community. In the grassland food web, for instance, wildebeests eat grasses. Lions, in turn, eat wildebeests.

Together, plants and animals pass energy through the biome community. They also use some of the energy to live. At each stage of the food web, some energy is lost as the animals use it. It is lost in the form of heat. More energy from the sun has to be trapped by plants to keep the community alive.

◇ 24 ◇

SOME PLANTS AND ANIMALS IN THE
GRASSLANDS FOOD WEB

PLANTS	HERBIVORES	CARNIVORES
Eaten by →	*Eaten by* →	
Grasses	Jackrabbits	Eagles
Black-eyed Susans	Prairie Dogs	Black-footed Ferets
Milkweed	Bison	Ferruginous Hawks
Prairie Blazing Star	Sparrows	Coyotes
Oaks	Pocket Gophers	Burrowing Owls
Cottonwoods	Prairie Chickens	Snakes
Willows	Grasshoppers	Foxes
		Lizards

SOIL LIFE

Beetles	Bacteria	Fungi	Lichens

Chapter 4

GRASSLAND PLANTS

As you might expect,
grasslands are mostly grass. But that does not
mean that all the grasses are the same. Even in one
patch of grass, many different kinds of grass
can be found. There are more than
11,000 types of grass in the world.
Tallgrass prairie is one type of
prairie of the Midwestern United States.
It is named for the tall grasses that grow

there. In tallgrass prairies, you can find big bluestem, which grows as high as 11 feet (3.4 meters) tall. But you may also find junegrass, buffalo grass, Canada wild rye, Indian grass, blue grama, little bluestem, porcupine grass, prairie cordgrass, and prairie dropseed.

Tropical grasslands usually have fewer kinds of grass. They may be made up of mostly one or two types.

The Shape of Grass

Grasses have special features that make them well prepared to grow in grassland environments. For one thing, they grow from the bottom up. Most plants, from wildflowers to trees, grow from the top: Their new growth is at the tips of stems and branches. But the new growth of grasses is at the base of their long leaves, or "blades." This allows grazing

Prairie cordgrass is one of the many grasses that grows in a tallgrass prairie.

animals to munch off the ends of their leaves without stopping the grasses' growth.

Grasses are adapted to survive the long dry season of the tropical grassland year. They can also survive several years of severe dryness, which may occur in any grassland. Most grasses, such as porcupine grass and blue grama, are perennials. Perennials live for several years. In the dry season,

Grazing animals, such as this warthog, eat the tops of the grass.

the parts of the grass above the soil turn yellow and die. But underneath, the deep roots store up energy for next year's growth. Growth buds are just below the surface, fairly safe from any fire or dryness. When the rain falls again, they can quickly grow. The grassland turns green again. Some tropical grasses can grow an inch each day.

You may not have noticed, but grasses have flowers. Small green bundles at the top of their stalks have dozens of tiny flowers on them in the rainy season or summer. Grasses rely mainly on the wind to bring the pollen of one flower to the next. Then the flowers can develop into seeds. Seeds help the grasses spread to new areas. Because grasses are pollinated by the wind, their flowers do not have to be showy to attract insect pollinators such as bees or butterflies.

The tops of this buffalo grass have many tiny flowers in bundles.

⬥ **29** ⬥

Black-eyed Susans and gloriosa daisies fill a grassland with color.

More Than Grass

Grasslands are not just grass, as you already know. Many other kinds of plants grow alongside the grasses, especially wildflowers in the sunflower and pea families. In the tallgrass prairies of North America, you can find milkweed, coneflower, stinging nettle, spiderwort, and others blooming in the summer. Prairie blazing stars shoot toward the big sky with spikes of magenta flowers, and black-eyed Susans nod in the breeze. Tropical grasslands usually have fewer wildflowers mixed in among the grasses.

There may also be trees in some grasslands. Box elder, oaks, and redbud trees grow among the grasses

Two large cottonwood trees fill out this grassland.

of North American prairies. Cottonwoods and willows spread along river valleys, where there is more water. In tropical grasslands, palms, pines, and acacias may be sprinkled

across the land. These trees grow fast, so they are soon tall enough to survive grassland fires. Tall grasses are also safe from browsing animals.

These flat-topped acacia trees grow in tropical grasslands.

◇ **31** ◇

✓ **Lots of grass:** There are more than 11,000 species of grass in the world.

✓ **Grow from bottom:** The new growth of grasses is at the base of their long leaves, preventing grazers or fires from stopping their growth.

✓ **More than grass:** Other kinds of plants grow alongside grasses, especially wildflowers in the sunflower and pea families.

GRASSLAND PLANTS

✓ **Wind flowers:** Grass flowers are pollinated mostly by the wind that blows across grasslands.

✓ **Many perennials:** Many grasses survive year after year, through dry periods and fires, in the form of their underground root masses.

✓ **A few trees:** Many grasslands also include some trees, either clustered around river valleys or sprinkled across the land.

GRASSLAND ANIMALS

The energy

stored in grasses and
other grassland
plants is used by many
grassland animals that make their home there.
These animals have special features for living
in grasslands, such as long legs for running
and extra stomach sections for digesting
grass. These animals continue the
grassland food web.

Eating Grass

Many grassland animals eat nothing but grass. In North America, bison, pronghorn antelope, and elk graze on prairie grasses. The Russian steppes are grazed by saiga antelope, wild horses called tarpans, and a cousin of the bison called the wisent. African grasslands are grazed by zebras and wildebeests.

Grass can be hard to digest. Large herbivores have special adaptations for eating grass. They have huge rear teeth for chewing the grass over and over.

Some of them, such as bison and antelope, have three or four chambers in their stomach. These hold special bacteria that help the animals break down the grass.

There are also smaller grass eaters. Grasshoppers, leaf-hoppers, beetles, and many other insects graze on one blade at a time. In North America, meadow voles, ground squirrels, black-tailed jackrabbits, and prairie dogs enjoy clumps of grass. In Africa, there are Cape hares, spring hares, and giant rats also known as grass cutters.

Grasshoppers eat one blade of grass at a time.

◇ **35** ◇

A black-tailed prairie dog munches on some grass.

More Plant Food

Other animals find different plant foods in grasslands. Bees visit prairie wildflowers for nectar and pollen. Butterflies, such as monarchs and western tiger swallowtails, also come to flowers for their nectar. These insects help bring pollen from one flower to another, allowing the flowers to make seeds.

Many animals eat seeds produced by grasses and other grassland plants. Seeds are packed with important nutrients that help these animals survive. Meadow voles and ground squirrels search for seeds on the ground. Birds, such as goldfinches, meadowlarks, and sparrows, eat seeds right off the plants.

Pocket gophers of North American grasslands eat mostly the roots of plants. They burrow under the ground until they find a tasty root. Then they eat the root in the safety of their burrow. If they really

Western meadowlarks eat grassland seeds.

like the plant, they may pull the shoots and leaves into their burrow to eat as well. The whole plant just disappears underground.

Some animals change their diet from plant food to animal food, depending on the season. These omnivores, such as greater prairie chickens, eat mostly leaves and seeds. But in the summer, they also eat their share of the abundant insects. Sandhill cranes eat everything from grass and seeds to insects, small mammals, and even the eggs of other birds.

Grassland Hunting

Carnivores continue the grassland food web by hunting and eating other animals. For example, Great Plains toads, fence lizards, and a bird called the

common snipe hunt for insects among the grass in North America. Kestrels, which are small falcons, swoop down on grasshoppers. Dragonflies dart through the air after flying insects.

Snakes, such as gopher snakes and racers, find plenty of rodents to eat in grasslands. Western hognose snakes use their upturned nose to burrow after toads, their favorite prey. Badgers hunt for rodents; they are expert at burrowing after them with their large, powerful claws. Burrowing owls hunt for small rodents, lizards, and birds, as well as insects. Ferruginous hawks and golden eagles hunt from the air, usually looking for larger prey like jackrabbits or prairie dogs.

A southern pocket gopher emerges from its burrow in Arizona.

A golden eagle hunts from the air for its next meal.

Black-footed ferrets, rare relatives of the weasel, hunt for prairie dogs. Hundreds of prairie dogs may live in networks of burrows called towns. The ferrets' long, low shape allows them to follow the prairie dogs down into their burrows.

Red foxes, swift foxes, and coyotes are the largest predators of North American prairies. They hunt for

jackrabbits, prairie dogs, and other small mammals and birds among the grass. Wolves once hunted for pronghorn, bison, and elk, but wolves are no longer found in the small areas of prairie left.

African herbivores, such as these zebras and wildebeests, travel together.

African Grasslands

African grasslands have the greatest number of large herbivores of any grassland. Zebras, gazelles, buffalo, wildebeests, and others graze together. They may move together to different areas each season, looking for the best grass. Because there are few trees or shrubs to hide among, these animals are safer from predators if they stay in large groups.

Elephants, giraffes, and black rhinos browse from the occasional trees and shrubs found in savannas. So do many antelope, such as impalas and eland. Warthogs eat grass and dig for bulbs and roots under the ground. In the case of elephants, each animal eats as much as 440 pounds (200 kilograms) of plant food every day.

This abundance of herbivores supports a similar assortment of carnivores. Lions, leopards, cheetahs, hunting dogs, hyenas, and jackals all prey on large herbivores. The energy from grassland plants flows through the herbivores to the carnivores.

Grasslands can support an amazing variety of animals. Scientists like Dave Balfour are trying to understand how large herbivores live together in grasslands and what they need to survive. This information will help park managers meet the needs of grassland wildlife and protect the grassland biome for the future.

Cheetahs chase down an impala in Kenya, Africa.

✓ **Grass eaters:** Many grassland animals, from leaf-hoppers to prairie dogs to bison, eat grass.

✓ **Plant food:** Other plant foods found by grassland animals include nectar, and seeds.

✓ **Tropical abundance:** African savannas have the greatest variety of large animals, including herbivores and predators.

GRASSLAND ANIMALS

✓ **Flexible diet:** Some animals, such as greater prairie chickens and sandhill cranes, may change their diet with the season, depending on what is available.

✓ **A feast of rodents:** Snakes, badgers, burrowing owls, sandhill cranes, and many other predators rely on the abundance of rodents in grasslands.

WORDS TO KNOW

adaptation—A trait that a plant or animal develops over time to help it live under certain conditions.

bacteria—Simple, one-celled life-forms that are helpful in breaking down plant matter into soil. Some bacteria help digest grass in the stomachs of some herbivores.

biome—An area of the earth defined by the kinds of plants that live there.

browser—An animal that eats leaves, buds, and twigs off trees or other woody plants.

carnivore—An animal that eats other animals.

climate—The average weather conditions in an area, usually measured over years. It includes temperature, precipitation, and wind speeds.

community—All the plants and animals living and interacting in any area.

decompose—The breakdown of dead plants and animals into soil.

decomposers—Soil animals, bacteria, and fungi that help break down dead plants and animals and release their nutrients back into the soil.

food web—The connections between plants and animals that allow the transfer of energy from the sun to plants to herbivores, carnivores, and decomposers.

grazer—An animal that eats grass.

herbivore—An animal that eats plants.

nutrients—Chemicals necessary for plants and animals to live and grow.

omnivore—An animal that eats both plants and other animals.

perennial—A plant that survives year after year, but may wait out the winter or dry season in the form of bulbs or roots under the ground.

prairie—A North American grassland.

predator—An animal that hunts other animals for food.

savanna—An area of mixed grassland and trees in Africa.

steppe—A grassland in Europe and Asia.

subtropical grassland—A grassland growing in warm regions, but not quite in the tropics, such as in South America.

temperate grassland—A grassland growing in cooler regions, like the North American prairies or the European and Asian steppes.

tropical grassland—A grassland growing near the equator, such as African velds and savannas.

BOOKS

Butterfield, Moira. *Looking at Animals on Plains and Prairies*. London: Chrysalis Books, 2000.

Cole, Melissa. *Prairies*. San Diego: Blackbirch Press, 2003.

Patent, Dorothy Hinshaw. *Life in a Grassland*. Minneapolis: Lerner Publications Company, 2003.

Stille, Darlene R. *Grasslands*. San Francisco: Children's Book Press, 2000.

Wallace, Marianne D. *America's Prairies and Grasslands: Guide to Plants and Animals*. Golden, Colo.: Fulcrum Publishing, 2001.

INTERNET ADDRESSES

USDA Forest Service. *National Grasslands.*
    http://www.fs.fed.us/grasslands/

Missouri Botanical Gardens. *Grasslands.* © 2002.
    http://mbgnet.mobot.org/sets/grasslnd/

INDEX